Wonders

Mc
Graw
Hill
Education

Cover: Nathan Love

mheducation.com/prek-12

Send all inquiries to:
McGraw-Hill Education
Two Penn Plaza
New York, New York 10121

ISBN: 978-0-07-906631-2
MHID: 0-07-906631-3

Printed in the United States of America.

3 4 5 6 7 8 QSX 23 22 21 20 19

A

Program Authors

Diane August

Donald R. Bear

Kathy R. Bumgardner

Jana Echevarria

Douglas Fisher

David J. Francis

Vicki Gibson

Jan Hasbrouck

Timothy Shanahan

Josefina V. Tinajero

Mc
Graw
Hill
Education

UNIT 1

Getting to Know Us

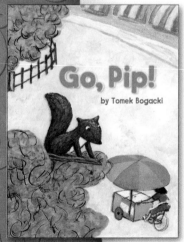

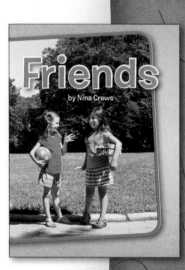

Essential Question

What do you do at your school?

Read about a boy who brings a special friend to school.

Go Digital!

6

Nat and Sam

by Pat Cummings

Nat is at **school**.

Nat sat.

What does Nat have?

cat
can
pan
tan
tap

Nat has Sam.

Nat does **not** have Sam!

Sam sat.

Sam is with Pam.

Look! Sam can read.

Can Nat? Nat can.

Nat and Sam like school.

Meet Pat Cummings

Pat Cummings moved a lot when she was growing up, so she understands why Nat would bring an old friend to a new place. She loves to draw and write stories. And like Nat and Sam, she loves to read a good book.

Author's Purpose

Pat Cummings wanted to tell a story about a boy and the things he does at school. Draw a picture of something you do at school.

©Marvin Lee

Respond to the Text

Retell

Use your own words to retell the important details in *Nat and Sam.*

Detail	Detail	Detail

Write

How do Nat's feelings about school change? Use these sentence frames:

I read that Nat feels...
I know that changes because...

Make Connections

What does Nat do that you can do at school, too?

ESSENTIAL QUESTION

Compare Texts

Read about how kids follow the rules at their school.

Rules at School

Ariel Skelley/Blend Images/Getty Images

Why do we have **rules** at school?

Rules can help us get along.
Rules can help us stay safe.

We raise our hands.

We listen quietly.

23

We **obey** **safety** rules.

We let everyone play!
What are your school rules?

Make Connections

Why is it important to have rules at school? **Essential Question**

Essential Question

What is it like where you live?

Read about a squirrel's day out in the city.

Go Digital!

26

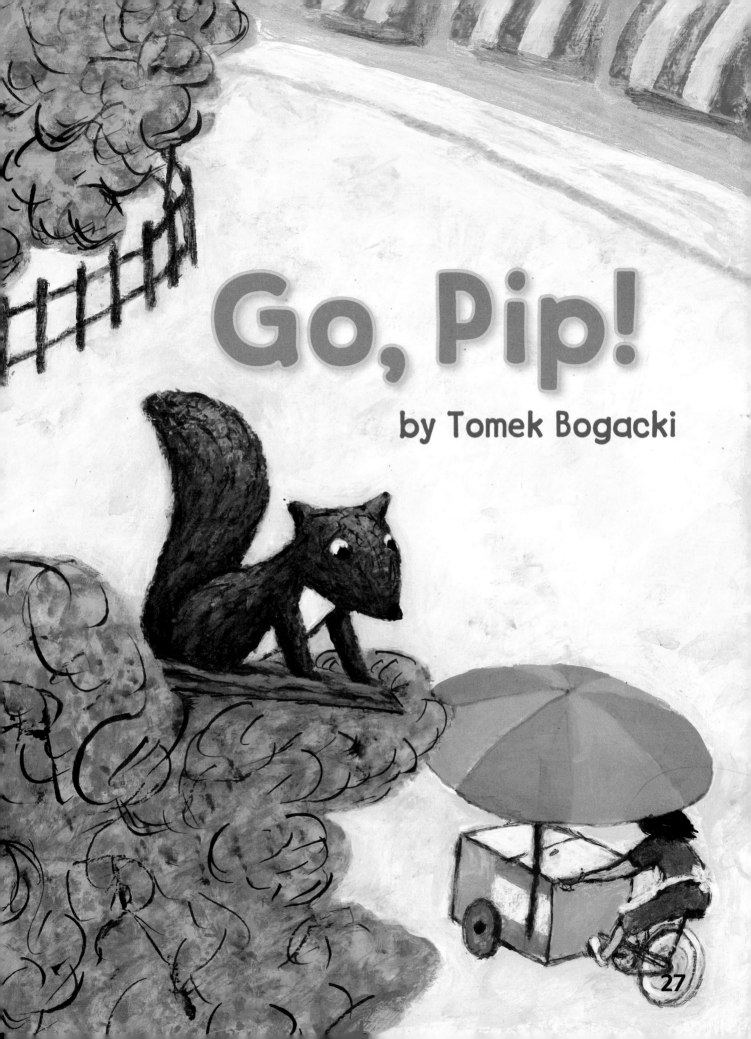

Go, Pip!

by Tomek Bogacki

Pip sits. Pip looks.

Pip can jump!

Pip is **out**.

Go, Pip!

Pip looks **up**.
It is **very** big.

Pip can look **down**.

Pip will go in.

Will this hat fit Pip?
It will!

Pip will go here.

Pip can look.

Where will Pip go?

Pip will go home!

Meet Tomek Bogacki

Tomek Bogacki used to live in a house in the forest. He liked to watch the animals there and draw pictures of them. Now he lives in a city where he likes to walk along the streets, visit museums, and watch squirrels in the park.

Author's Purpose

Tomek Bogacki wanted to tell a story about a curious squirrel who visits a city. Draw an animal visiting where you live. What might it see there?

Tomek Bogacki

40

Respond to the Text

Retell

Use your own words to retell the important details in *Go, Pip!*

Detail	Detail

Write

Describe how where Pip lives affects what he does. Use these sentence starters:

I read that Pip...
The words and illustrations help me know that Pip...

Make Connections

What other fun things could Pip do in a city?

ESSENTIAL QUESTION

Read Together

Compare Texts

Read about what it's like to live in the city.

A Surprise in the City

Hi! My name is Zoë.
I live in the **city**.
This is my **building**.

I look out my window.
I am excited!
Mom has a surprise for me today.

We go to the **playground**.
I play on the swings.
Is **this** my surprise?
Mom says no.

I learn a new jump at gymnastics.
Is **this** my surprise?
Mom says no.

Mom buys me a pretzel.
Is **this** my surprise?
Mom says no.

We stop at the pencil store.
This is my surprise!
I buy lots of pencils.
I **love** my surprise!

 Make Connections

What is similar about the
places Zoë and Pip visit?

Essential Question

Essential Question

What makes a pet special?

Read about a very unusual pet who goes to school.

Go Digital!

FLIP

by Ezra R. Tanaka

illustrated by
Michael Garland

Flip is my pet.
Flip is big.

Flip can not go in.
Flip is sad.

Flip **pulls** me in.

Flip and I go to class.

Flip sits.
Be good, Flip!

Flip likes class.

The kids like Flip.

Miss Black is mad.
Sit down, Flip!

Look at Miss Black!

Flip has a plan.

Flip did it!
The class claps.

Can Flip **come** back?
"Flip can," said Miss Black.
Flip is glad!

Meet the Illustrator

When Michael Garland was a child, he loved drawing characters from movies and books. Some of his favorite movies and books had funny creatures in them. So he drew a lot of dinosaurs just like Flip!

Illustrator's Purpose

Michael Garland likes to draw dinosaurs. Draw a dinosaur. Label your drawing.

Michael Garland

Respond to the Text

Use your own words to retell three important details in *Flip*. Tell the details in order.

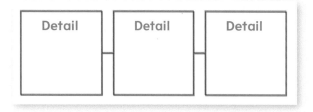

Detail	Detail	Detail

Write

Write a story about what happens when you take a make-believe pet to school. Use these sentence frames:

My make-believe pet is a...
My pet is very...

Make Connections COLLABORATE

How is Flip special?
ESSENTIAL QUESTION

63

Genre Nonfiction

Compare Texts

Read about how to give pets what they need.

iguana

What Pets Need

What do pets **need**?

parrot

hamster

Like all **living things**, pets need food.
Some pets eat seeds or plants.

kittens

Some pets eat meat or fish.
All pets need fresh water.

dog

Pets need a safe home.
Pets need our love and **care**.

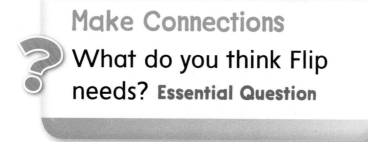

Make Connections

? What do you think Flip
needs? **Essential Question**

Genre Nonfiction

Essential Question

What do friends do together?

Read about how two friends have fun together.

Go Digital!

Nina Crews

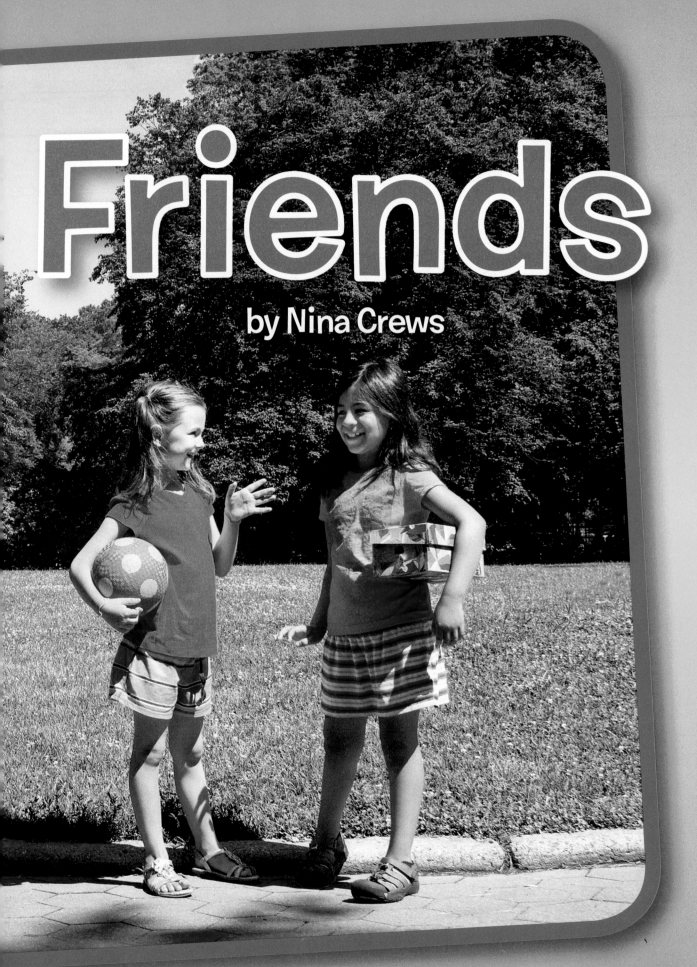

Friends

by Nina Crews

© Nina Crews

Pam and Jill are friends.
They play a lot.

Pam and Jill toss a ball.

Pam hops.
Jill hops, **too**!

72

They play tag.
Pam is quick.

Jill is not as quick as Pam.

Jill is hot.
She does not like tag.

75

Pam **makes** a plan.
She has a box.

Jill looks in.
It is a doll and a dog!

Pam and Jill sit on a rock.
They make up a game.

The dog and doll are friends.

Pam and Jill play, play, play.

It is a **fun** day!

Meet Nina Crews

Nina Crews uses photographs to tell stories about children. The children in the photographs are her family or friends. She says that her readers like to see pictures of real children.

Nina Crews

Author's Purpose

Nina Crews wanted to tell about real things friends do when they play together. Draw a picture of you and a friend playing.

Respond to the Text

Retell

Use your own words to retell three important details in *Friends*.

Detail	Detail	Detail

Write

How does Pam's plan change the way the girls play together? Use these sentence frames:

> At the beginning, Pam and Jill...
> Pam's plan...

Make Connections

COLLABORATE

What can friends do when they want to play different games?

ESSENTIAL QUESTION

There Are Days And There Are Days

by Beatrice Schenk de Regniers

There are days I want to be
all alone
with only me
for company—
me and my cat.
There <u>are</u> days like that.

And there are days
(many more)
I don't want to be alone
any more.
Then
it seems to me
jokes are funnier,
honey's honey-er,
sun is sunnier
when
I'm with a friend!

Make Connections
What does the boy
like about being
with a friend?
Essential Question

Illustration: Courtney A. Martin

85

Genre Nonfiction

Essential Question

How does your body move?

Read about the fun ways kids can move.

Go Digital!

Read Together

Move It!

How can kids **move**?
We can move in lots of ways.
We use our bodies to help us.

I can **run**.
I have strong legs.
They help me go fast.

legs

feet

I can **jump**.
I pick up my feet.
I will land on the grass.

I can catch.
I use **two** hands.
I can grab the ball.

hands

89

feet

arms

I can swim.
I pull with my arms.
I kick with my feet.

I can spin this hoop.
I move my hips fast.
This helps it stay up.

hips

I can do fun tricks.
There are lots of ways to move!
What can you do?

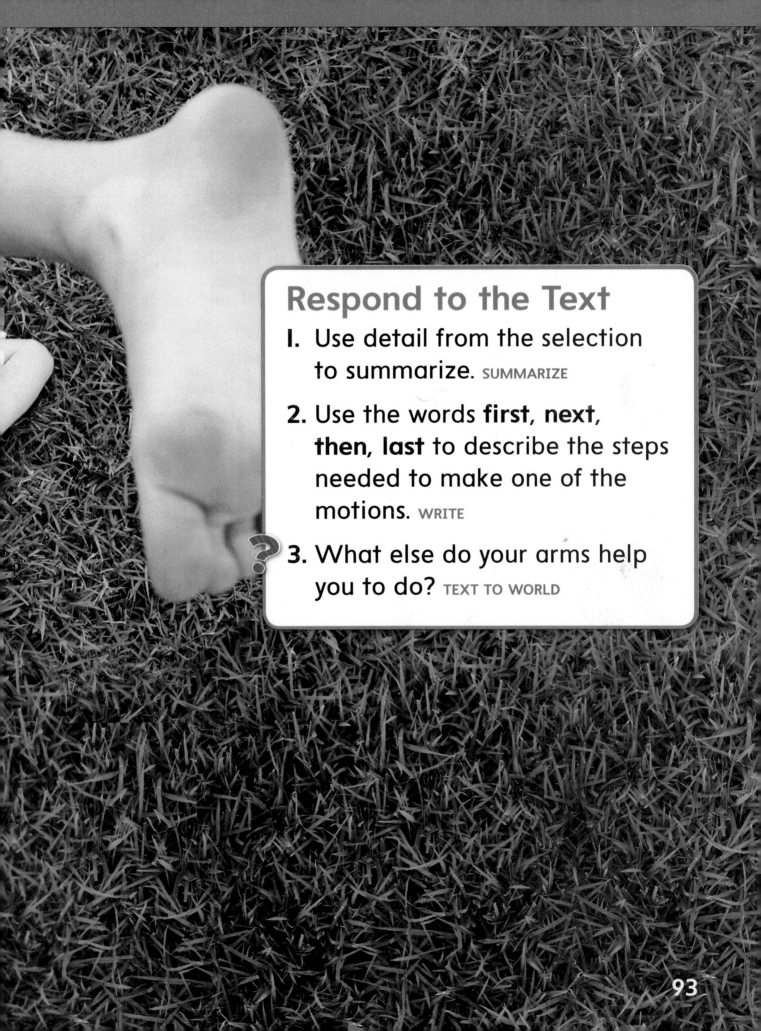

Respond to the Text

1. Use detail from the selection to summarize. SUMMARIZE

2. Use the words **first**, **next**, **then**, **last** to describe the steps needed to make one of the motions. WRITE

3. What else do your arms help you to do? TEXT TO WORLD

Compare Texts

Read about how one family likes to move.

My Family Hike

Hi! My name is Otto.
Today I'm going **hiking**.
I will look for snakes on the trail.
I grab my hat and water bottle.

We drive to the trail.
My sister and I want to be first.
I **start** to look for snakes.
I search for anything moving.

Soon I'm hot and out of **breath**.
I **climb** on a rock to get a better view.
I see a snake!
It slips away and hides near a tree.

Finally we stop.
There are tall trees all around us.
We made it to the top of the mountain!
I will look for **another** snake!

 Make Connections

How does this family like to move?

Essential Question

Marques/Shutterstock.com

Glossary

What is a Glossary? A glossary can help you find the meanings of words. The words are listed in alphabetical order. You can look up a word and read it in a sentence. Sometimes there is a picture to help you.

Sample Entry

Letter

Hh

Main Entry

Sentence

hop

The bunny can **hop**.

Bb

big

A hippo is **big**.

Cc

clap

Kim and Roz **clap**.

Dd

doll

I hug my **doll**.

Gg

good

This is **good** for me.

Hh

hat
This **hat** is red.

hop
The bunny can **hop**.

Mm

move
We **move** around and around.

Pp

pull
We **pull** on the rope.

Rr

run
It is fun to **run** in a race.

Ss

school
Our **school** is very big.

sit

The kids **sit** in a circle.

Tt

trick

We can see the **trick**.